P A U S E.

J. R. Carpenter is a queer artist, writer, mudlark, fossil hunter, and a lecturer at University of Leeds. Born of migrants in Mi'kma'ki they lived in Tiohtià:ke for many years before emigrating to England in 2010. Their work asks questions about place, displacement, colonialism, and climate across performance, print and digital media. For more information visit luckysoap.com

Also by J. R. Carpenter

Measures of Weather (Shearsman Books, 2025)

Le plaisir de la côte / The Pleasure of the Coast (Pamenar Press, 2023)

City of Marvels (Broken Sleep Books, 2023)

Words for Worlds Upended (Guillemot Press, 2020)

This is a Picture of Wind (Longbarrow Press, 2020)

A General History of the Air (above/ground press, 2020)

An Ocean of Static (Penned in the Margins, 2018)

The Gathering Cloud (Uniformbooks, 2017)

GENERATION[S] (Traumawein, 2010)

Words the Dog Knows (Conundrum Press, 2008)

CONTENTS

p a u s e. 11

Acknowledgements 130

© 2026, J. R. Carpenter. All rights reserved. No part of this book may be reproduced, stored in a retrieval system, or transmitted in any form or by any means, whether electronic, mechanical, photocopying, recording, or otherwise, without the prior written permission of the publisher, except in the case of brief quotations used in reviews or scholarly works.

This work may not be used for text and data mining, including (without limitation) the training of artificial intelligence technologies or systems. The author and publisher expressly reserve all rights and opt out of any applicable text and data mining exceptions.

ISBN: 978-1-917617-56-7

Cover designed by Aaron Kent

Edited and Typeset by Aaron Kent

The author has asserted their right to be identified as the author of this Work in accordance with the Copyright, Designs and Patents Act 1988

Broken Sleep Books Ltd
PO BOX 102
Llandysul
SA44 9BG

*for Christine Stewart and notokwew muskwa manitokan
(old woman bear sitting next to the creator)*

p a u s e.

J. R. Carpenter

Broken Sleep Books

What I'm wondering is this:
can a simple act of attention be called political?

— Kathleen Jamie, 'Lissen Every Thing Back'. 2019

pause.

an interval. of inaction.
especially due. to hesitation.

a break. in speaking.
or reading. or writing.

[this page. has been left blank. with intention.]

||

a control. or button.

allowing. the interruption.

of the operation. of a recording.

or playback. device.

||

to wait. upon.

to linger. over.

a break.

away from.

looking. watching. gazing.

hearing. hungry listening.

hungry listening proceeds without pause

    — Dylan Robinson, *Hungry Listening.* 2020: 215

II

people keep asking me.
how it feels to be back.

in this place.
I've never been.

Canada, I guess they mean.
but what does that mean.

> a fictive coherence. (Dallas Hunt, *Creeland*. 2021: 62)
> an act of imagination. (Jeffers Lennox, *Homelands and Empires*. 2017: 3)

I am a migrant. a double emigrant.

born of immigrants. born of emigrants.

this is the furthest inland.

I've been in some time.

||

two weeks. in quarantine.
learning. what dry smells like.

learning. the difference. between.
conifers. fir. spruce. and pine.

two weeks. of heat. and bright. and then.
the sky darkening. the thunder rumbling.

a close crow. calling.
a small plane. passing.

wind lifts. air freshens.
mineral. drops. of rain.

the close crow. rises.
something starts. ending.

and also.
a beginning.

II

fourteen days to the minute.
okay I admit it. minus a few.

bolt. through the side gate.
at last! past the edge. of the lawn.

>   cross the ocean. cross the country.
>   cross the crosswalk. cross the grass.

first foot to the path. slipping. in slick thick sticky.
bentonite, I think. gumbo, they call it, in Wyoming.

first foot forward. steps. into a past place.
an extraction. economy. of nomenclature.

>   low yields. high grit content.
>   thick. overburden. reduces desirability.
>   (D. W. Scafe, *Alberta Bentonites*)

| |

heart. racing. feet.
a flight. of stairs. surprisingly steep.

a river. lives across the street from me.
kisiskâciwanisîpiy. from nêhiyawêwin.

for swift-flowing. water running.
under. out. of language.

from the pedestrian bridge.
voices clatter. across jade water.

talk to me. about.
where this bridge is.

exactly.

II

people keep trying to tell me. Edmonton is a city.
the scale. of this place. eludes me.

amiskwaciwâskahikan. from nêhiyawêwin.
for beaver hills house.

and indeed. there are beavers. building houses.
within walking distance. from the house.

I am renting. I am visiting.
I am listening. I am glimpsing.

occasional glints. of glass and steel.
rising. through poplars.

a corner garden. a blaze.
of cosmos. and chrysanthemum.

a false sky. of blue tarpaulin.
bright. against the wildfire haze.

a confusion. of figure and forest.
city and field.

II

scrambling. down a non-path.
skirting. a soft edge.

squatting. to examine.
a conglomeration. of pebbles.

suspended. in strata. of sandstone.
slide scars. over coal seams.

shale beds. thrust faults.
and bands. of concretions.

hard solid masses.
the local accumulation.

of matter.
within sediment.

II

wind gusting. to gale force. at a place.
they call. the end of the world.

dust-sized. shards swirl.
ellipsoidal fragments. of pumice.

created by the Bridge River eruption.
of the Mount Meager massif.

carried eastward. by prevailing winds.
2,350 years ago. or so.

Alexander the Great had just defeated the Persians.
what I'm saying is. even this dust. is a settler.

No geology is neutral.

    — Kathryn Yusoff, *A Billion Black Anthropocenes or None.* 2018

11

an active. hesitation.
between. wanting. and taking.

making. the taking.
into something. different.

II

a silence.

an offering.

an act. or instance.

of acknowledging.

> a land acknowledgment is not enough.
> (Joseph Pierce, *HYPERALLERGIC*. 2022)

a. knowledge. meant.

giving. something.

back.

| |

attention. a tension.
attend. to tend.

a pact. a performance.
a set. of instructions:

>	go outside. every day.
>	pay attention.
>
>	until you notice something.
>	you want to tell. another person.

11

colder. barer. birches. slender. silver.
arms flail. under a flat matt foil. of sky.

a patter. a splatter. a smattering of rain.
scattering sound. down. the stairs. to the river.

outstanding. the way some small pebbles.
float to the surface. and perch.

mudstone. eroding out from under them.
small alters. proffering. long-buried gems.

flecks of light. at right angles. pyrite crystals.
in quartzite. fools gold. a fools errand, this.

freezing fingers. river dipped. to wash. a stone.
to hold. the light. a complicated unit. of magic.

11

the sky brightening. broadening. to threadbare blue.
a blaze. of leaves. golden. glowing. throwing.

flecks of sun. on the water. on the feathers.
of the wet ducks. blown backwards.

flapping forwards.
hard. to stay.

in one place.

11

a sky undecided. about colour. -- *it* was the colour.
of mutton-fat jade, Elizabeth Bishop writes.

of sea, or of sky? I can't remember. and anyway.
that was March. and this is October. and this is a river.

not sure either. if mutton-fat is Bishop's phrase.
or the jade's. or how closely. the semi-precious.

stone actually resembles. animal fat.
or the difference. between fat and flesh.

it was cold and windy, she writes. scarcely the day.
to take a walk on that long beach. but here we are.

damp. scattered stones. throwing long shadows.
another echo. and water cold. as knowledge must be.

that salt sea. distracting me. from this fresh. now.
something slides sideways. suspiciously like snow.

11

steep. wooden steps. creaking. with cold.
shivering. timber. sounds. of a ship.

last sprigs. of red. rowan berry. and leaf.
flair. against black spruce. trunks.

and silver stands. of birch.
and purple thistle. still in flower.

a dense. blue. sky to the north.
a grim. grey. westerly.

gathering. in the bottom.
of a large. cumulous.

rising. over the soft stone of the cliff.
rising. over a sandy bit. of the beach.

shifting. into a pebble stretch. a shelf. of low coal.
crumbling. into sand. or mud. or clay. or silt.

II

a day at odd angles.
skews the spruce sideways.

a dry of eye. an ache of head.
a bark of birch. a thin of skin.

a patch of grass. a whorl of hair.
a pile of logs. a cold of bones.

but then. a clearing. after.
a spell of warm. a sun of needles.

||

dazzle sky steers me. sparkle snow veers me.
southwest. a way I've never been.

path walks behind me. light sees through me.
cold focuses me. sharp frames me.

curvaceous blades. of dried grasses.
curled leaves. of wild roses.

red berries. bend slender branches.
copper leaves. freeze before falling.

in the half-light. of evening.
the larches. let down their long hair.

11

a trio of trumpeter swans. stands on a ledge.
of thin ice. at the edge. of the river.

swans. standing. on ice. feels profoundly wrong.
after a decade. as a migrant. in England.

I realise. I've internalised. colonial attitudes.
about geese leaving. and swans standing.

I blame the Queen.

the Crown of England. has held the right. to claim ownership of unmarked mute swans swimming in

open waters since the twelfth century, when swans were a prized food. served at feasts and banquets.

trumpeter swans are indigenous to Great Turtle Island. they weigh twenty-five pounds and have a wingspan of

two metres. they need a runway of a hundred metres of open water to lift their heavy bodies into flight.

in the seventeenth century, their long flight feathers were coveted for hats and writing quills.

aggressive conservation. has helped.
bring them back. from near extinction.

II

river ice budding.
not yet blooming.
cracking. booming.

trees creaking.
speaking.
their own language.

intricate.
some wounds.
are clearly deliberate.

geese amassing.
where the river bows.
westwards.

hearts racing.
southwards.
towards a temporary home.

II

mild. bordering on humid. for here.
late. for a first. walking. date. with a Treaty Rights lawyer.

niya nôtokêw maskwa manitokan
old woman bear sitting next to the creator.

where are you from? she squints at me.
as ever. I have no idea. how to answer.

Nova Scotia, New York, Hungary, Montreal, England?
well, this is my territory, she says. and spreads her arms.

she tells me she grew up four hundred miles downriver.
in Saskatchewan? I don't use those names, she says.

what's the river like, four hundred miles from here?
wider, she says.

the path we want is closed.
we discuss our options.

she doesn't know what I mean.

by the place they call The End of the World.

I don't know about the road that came before The End.

it was fun to drive, she says.

11

we walk past a log cabin. the white mud. between the logs.
has volcanic ash in it, so it dries into a hard clay, she says.

I've been reading about the specific volcano.
the eruption. that this ash came from, I say.

we agree that 2,350 years ago feels recent.
for an eruption.

geologists say the river formed 12,000 years ago.
post glaciation.

they say, she says.
aye. all rivers are recent.

people are stories.
and stories are ancient.

11

old woman bear teaches me the difference.
between high bush cranberries. and wild mountain ash.

oh, I thought those were rowan berries.
we don't have anything called rowan here, she says.

my phone informs us. that wild mountain ash.
and rowan. are two names. for the same thing.

much discussion ensues.
about jellies and syrups.

depending on the time of year, the berries of wild
mountain ash, or rowan, can be exceptionally bitter
due to the presence of sorbic acid. named after the
scientific name for the genus, Sorbus. Parasorbic acid is
also present, which causes indigestion and could cause
kidney damage. Parasorbic acid is broken down when
heated. the fruit must be cooked before use.

11

the sky blues before us.
the sun warms behind us.

old woman bear teaches me.
the word for sun. pîsim.

it sounds like peace.
and ends in the front of the mouth.

| |

the sky lapis. a lapsus.
a slip of warmth. a spell of trees.

the north wind. shakes. branches.
loose. of the last. of the leaves.

the river. a massive mass. of contradictions.
or maybe dialectics. dialogues between.

frozen and flooded. solid and shattered.
swift and still. silver and silt.

the river ice. never moving.
when out walking.

have yet to catch it.
cracking / rucking // buckling ///

so when then. does it happen.
this sheering / slicing // piling ///

II

ice autocorrects. to I've on my phone.
I've formed in the river. I've frozen eyelashes.

I've encased slender branches. succumbed in spots.
slicked the path. dripped. in low slung.

sun. lights. the last. of the grasses.
long shadows. spill sideways. even at noon.

blue bruises. pool. in shade shallows.
air bubbles. under thin. ice. skin.

snow. less cold. than it looks.
blue gloves. not lips.

rose hips. make good jelly.
high bush cranberries.

will save your life.
if necessary.

||

a twig nest. lodged in a sky tress.
a wasps nest. dangles by a leaf stem.

a massive bird. of prey. perches.
on a high branch. over the ravine.

having seen one. I now seek others.
in absences. between branches.

sky-shaped spaces.
where wings could open.

11

a solitary crow. atop a tall spruce.
unfolds into. gives chase unto.

an even larger. raptor. of some sort.
a falcon maybe. white. under belly.

lifting. diving. banking.
harrying. fleeing. following.

never quite catching.
a fierce pas de deux.

11

the poplars' last stand.
the asters' ghost flowers.

it's the clinging on that I admire.
the autumn's last hurrah.

the fluff. the puff.
the almost.

but not quite. ready.
soon. to be flight.

11

a golden drop. of spruce gum.
shining in mild sun.

old woman bear insists. we chew some.
we spend the rest of the walk. prying it from our molars.

that was dumb, she says, after a while.
we won't have sore throats though, I reason.

in the zoo across the river. an elephant named Lucy.
would like to retire. but the zoo says she's too old to travel.

they have buffalo too, old woman bear says.
if they want to leave. they will.

II

three beaches. of morning.
three skies. of earlier.

three spruce shapes. in pink sunrise.
innumerable blue holes. torn in cirrostratus.

a grey horizontal. where one ought not to be.
an eroding contrail, possibly.

three varieties. of wings bright.
fir light. leaf frost. and feather flight.

11

queer larches.
deciduous conifers.

a cluster of cones. is as close.
as late November comes. to flowers.

never having been. on a first name basis.
with a larch before.

never knowingly having had the pleasure.
of basking in one's shadow.

I marvel. at this carpet. of gold glitter.
needle litter. taking a shine. to snow.

II

struggling. with a false sense. of sameness.

the river. piled over. with ice. and snow.

white is not nothing. not neutral. this blanket.

of muffle. this smoothing. over danger.

11

how many times. can I photograph. these same trees.
many. many times. it seems.

looking. not. for something new.
but with. the always different.

light. ever shifting. shading. colouring.
shaping shadow trees. lengthening. doubling.

II

the traffic noise. from the ring road.
feels especially present. on still days.

learning. to discern something.
akin to silence. beneath that noise.

and then. listening there. for what.
sounds emerge. within that silence.

learning. to listen for. or to.
or towards. or with. the birds.

> learning to lean into. the unfamiliar.
> the uncertainty of radical difference
> (Dylan Robinson, *Hungry Listening.* 2020: 216)

11

sitting. listening. to two birds chattering.
high in a pine. way over my head.

no way to ask them. what kind of birds they are.
who their kin are. where they come from.

where they live.
what they eat.

    who-cooks-for-you. who-cooks-for-you-all.
    the barred owl asks. every evening.

II

went out without my camera.

by which I mean, my phone.

decided not to go back for it.

then felt for it. (in my pocket). at least four times.

so much. of how I write.

is filtered. through the sequential.

a series. of visual compositions.

walking is pausing. stilling. framing.

> When I walk without a camera, my own shutter opens, and the moment's light prints on my own silver gut.
>
> (Annie Dillard, *Pilgrim at Tinker Creek*. 1974: 33)

try going out without a camera more often.

I note. but do not. do.

11

the snow shows. a fresh trail.
the width of a single. fat tire.

dipping. over the lip. and down.
round steep. hairpin curves.

the only way. not to slip. is to run.
that's how the bikes do it then. speed!

11

two weeks shy of solstice. what scant sun there is.
spills sideways. bare trees bask. in an orange glow.

it's old snow. shot through. with melt arteries.
veins of red dogwood. red brush. red willow.

the real cold. is coming. everyone assures me.
it's only. just slightly. delayed.

early evening. crampons biting. into ice gleaming.
under streetlights. holiday lights. garish. glaring.

save for one. perfectly shaped. perfectly lit.
white light. pine tree. a gift to the community.

11

how easily. days become jumbled.
writing into. tomorrow. referring.

to the day after. which is today.
yesterday. already. nearly. forgotten.

walking to the library. to pick up a book.
ordered weeks. if not months ago.

Carson. *If Not, Winter: Fragments of Sappho*.
I decide to assume. it's a manual.

open to a random page:
do not move stones. oh.

II

dates.

stones.

anchors.

bones.

all walking.

is listening now.

a pause. in music.

is a mark. over a note. or rest.

that is. to be.

l e n g t h e n e d .

11

walking and talking.
with old woman bear.

moving. only slightly faster.
than the lichen. at times.

sitting on a bench. near the beginning.
of a long story. still unfolding.

our thinking. spreading. further. wider.
an ongoing exchange. of listening.

11

a razzle of dogwood. a dazzle of light.
a stand of birch. a sky of bright.

ravens. close and numerous.
clamorous. except when silent.

on one thumb. a chickadee perches.
pauses. poses with a peanut.

increasingly pressing questions.
from friends in non-chickadee nations.

how do you… how long…
I mean, do you just…

| |

considering compiling a field guide.
but to what.

walking. with ears instead of eyes.
standing. with hands open.

inviting. the touch. of other creatures.
listen. they find you.

then. the thrum.
breath into lungs.

wings into air.

11

I see lots of bird feeders along here, a man stops to tell me.
I've never seen a single bird at any of them, he adds wistfully.

I put a suet feeder out, he says. no birds come.
I just saw two downy woodpeckers at a suet feeder, I say.

do you ever hear woodpeckers, he asks.
he never hears any.

his wife suggests I take the chickadee walk.
it's about an hour from here. she can't remember where.

I take a chickadee walk every day, I say.
where, they want to know.

at this point I start to wonder.
if maybe they're very wealthy.

11

as soon as they walk away.

a chickadee feeding frenzy ensues. in the palm of my hand.

and look, there's a pine grosbeak. there's another.

and further along. two white-breasted nuthatches.

more grosbeaks. more woodpeckers. more chickadees.

magpies. and over. and above us. ravens galore.

11

the park. mostly empty. except. what does empty mean.
for the poplar. black spruce. and Doug fir nations.

    the Douglas. named for a Scottish botanist.
    is not a true fir, spruce, or pine. nor is it a hemlock.

the park. mostly full then. of trees. of sky. of cold. of snow.
full of creak. full of boot. full of foot. full of fur. full of wool.

and the ravens. so close. I can hear their feathers. unfolding.
like the rustling. of weighted. silk gowns.

    feeling a bit queasy about resorting to simile.
    an unkindness. of Victorian mourning gowns.

11

walking. with old woman bear. along a stretch. of river.
where ravens gather. on high. bare branches.

there's no one word in English, I say.
for the sound. of wings. unfolding. rustling.

black and ragged. tree to tree. reminding me.
Joni Mitchel was born in Treaty 6 Territory.

that's pitihkwêkâstan, old woman bear says.
now I want to learn nêhiyawêwin.

> a language that listens to the world.
> and loves it. (Christine Stewart)

11

sun enough. standing.

basking. in an orange glow.

cold enough. walking. crunching.

hard snow. sounds hollow.

||

black sesame seeds. make.
black-capped chickadees.

black sky holes. make.
raven-shaped. absences.

side-eye. from papaschase.
the piliated woodpecker.

a straight-up pterodactyl.
kik-kik-kik-kik-kik (rate & pitch rise then fall).

and up on the ridge. the sky a blue. by Giotto.
and back at the house. hours spent. wondering.

if referencing Giotto. is a colonial imposition.
on this actual sky. so laden. with stars.

11

the glare before the sight.

the river before the ice.

the ice before the snow.

the snow before the blue.

the blue before the sky.

the walk before the sun.

the sun before the set.

the cold before the cold-cold.

comes closing in.

11

minus thirty-eight. with the wind.
minus twenty-seven. without.

but we are never. without
what can we do. without. feeling.

fingers. inside liner gloves. inside mitts.
cold. at the pit. at the back. of the knee.

can we do. without. feeling. sun on skin.
if that touch freezes. flesh. within minutes.

but the bright. but the light. but the sun.
the libidinal brain. endeavours to deceive us.

without. cloud cover. to hold. heat in.
a stand. of poplars. rises.

into a dome. of deep.
mineral blue.

11

can we do. without. feeling.
the touch. of other creatures.

a clutch. of claw. a fan. of feathers.
behind glasses. behind goggles.

a bat. of eye.
an opening. of lashes.

||

minus thirty-six. with the wind.
moving. a wave. of fine snow.

over. small dunes. of solid snow.
over. the jumbled ice.

over. the river. swift-flowing.
under. the ice. over. the silt.

spindrift. they call this.
wave blown mist. in England.

spoondrift. they call this. in Scotland.
ocean-going words. for colonial mists.

well inland. old woman bear teaches me.
papêskwacistin. referring specifically.

to the fine snow. drifting.
like a wave. moving.

over the rest of the snow.
scouring. polishing. smoothing.

11

minus twenty-seven. with the wind.
doesn't feel warmer. than minus thirty-seven.

in the sun. in the thrall. of the blue.
of a sky. bright as maybe. but then.

it clouded over. when I wasn't looking.
started snowing. minuscule. nearly invisible.

flakes. disappearing. in the flat light.
confusing. figure and field.

a downy woodpecker. glances.
over its shoulder. if birds have shoulders.

into a near distance. into which. I am encroaching.
in the foreground. a chickadee. anticipates flight.

a fluff. of undercarriage. incoming.
a whorl. of wing. of leaving.

11

feathers. are made. of keratin.
the same material. as fingernails.

each. a hollow quill.
attached to a muscle.

ideal for sky.
writing.

II

minus twenty-seven. with the wind.
so we keep out of it.

feel the grip of it.
loosening.

gloves off. in the valley.
feeding chickadees.

      chik-a-dee-dee-dee (rapid)

and exchanging greetings.
with downy woodpeckers.

      peeeeeeek (descending horse whinny)

bohemian waxwings.
white-breasted nuthatches.

      yank yank yank (sung through your nose)

and a raven. on the way back.

black as anything.

      cruck (harsh, raspy)

attacking a bin bag.

by the side. of Groat Road.

      tawk (metallic)

11

a morning. leaning.
towards warming.

a bare. of branch.
a tatter. of blue.

a slab. of solid.
a gleam. of future.

a spring. of river.
a soon. of melt.

a track. of bird.
a trail. of tail.

a bed. of snow.
a pine. of needles.

||

this orange hour.
a half moon over.

a flame. of sky.
one degree over.

zero.
a relief.

bordering.
on embrace.

11

six degrees. mostly sunny.
chickadees. mostly flirting.

blue sky. thick with ravens.
the sound. of cruck. cruck. croaking.

a dense cloud. of ravens. rises up.
in the shape of a raven.

a series. of oil paintings.
of sombre skies. ensues.

is there's a word. for when there are so many ravens.
they form a cloud the shape of a raven. flying.

I ask old woman bear. questions. about nêhiyawêwin.
when English. feels inadequate. to the specificities. of here.

she replies: kamâmawipayitwaw pîwâyisak.
birds flying together like a wave.

11

a hunger. of chickadee.
fluttering. around me.

a fondness. of peanut.
a fandom. of fungus.

a veneration. of lichen.
an abundance. of alone-time.

resulting. in a compulsion.
towards the creation.

of collective nouns.

11

I meet a 10-year-old in the park.

we both have chickadees. on our heads.

we stand. and compare notes.

about having chickadees on our heads.

II

put the bin out. and keep going.
out the back way. down the alley way.

walking. through fresh snow. falling.
following. an extremely. high frequency.

an earful. of bodies.
a static. of waxwings.

>   zeee-zeee-zeee (rapid)
>   always in flocks.

electric. in the phone lines.
high pitched. high wire. acts.

raising questions. about speed and stillness.
near and distance. the scant difference.

between dark clouds. and yellow linings.
silver underbellies. and pewter skies.

11

sluggish. from not sleeping.
eating. into morning.

a long day. of admin.
and the body's. inner workings.

watching. a friend. in another city.
typing. into a shared google doc.

>mom got hacked and conned
>fish got the ick died

watching. and wondering.
at this exhausted. typing.

>how come yrnotsleeping? she asks.
>wanting. to fix. to help. toholdeverybody.

how to create space. when the space bar.
only works. intermittently.

      have to hit right on it

how to mend.

      and hard

through fracture.

11

hearing before seeing.
a trumpeter swan returning.

here's the sky it flew through.
it's hollow. nasal honking. still audible.

here's the sound. of ice melting.

here's a contrail.
the flight of something larger.

here's me. hatless. squinting.
into blue distance.

here's a gathering. on the ridge.
waiting. on a sun. set. on setting.

it will soon be very beautiful. a man says.
making a nothing. of now.

| |

unaccustomed. to walking.
anywhere other. than the river valley.

yesterday. I forgot my wallet.
today. I misplaced the sky. amidst tall buildings.

weeping. this morning. in a workshop. on the epistolary.
then walking. from sap seeping. tree to tree.

dense stands. of spruce. birch. and poplars.
keeping. the city. out on a limb.

warm sun. slowly.
sinking in.

11

walking. weather hovering.
between mukluk. and wellington.

sweating. under one layer. too many.
but basking anyway. in sun. warm skin.

listening. to moving. river ice. melting.
is this progress. this impending. absence.

this dripping. this shattering.
a woodpecker. rat-a-tat. cracking.

beetle-dead. branches. silver. with lichen.
layers. of wet. of bark. of wood. of silt. of wing.

witnessing. the wounds. where ice came. crashing.
downriver. gashing. living spruce. standing. still.

noticing. contested boundaries. between bark and not.
leaf and rot. marvelling. at mud. in this dry place.

the amount of blue it takes. to hold these folds.
the amount of white. it takes. up space.

what is this. sky trying. to hide.
a solar halo. barely discernible.

a hollow. at the base. of an elm tree.
the creaks. and groans. of two elm trees.

leaning. chafing. scraping. growing. into one another.
the ongoing violence. of this long embrace.

no one. wants. to move. this slowly.

11

solar halo. over silver river.
folklore says. colder days ahead.

forecast says warmer. on this.
not even. the ravens. agree.

we hear you, we hear you, old woman bear tells them.
though these days. mostly. all we hear. is honking.

what's good for the goose. is having a gander.
geese mate for life, old woman bear says.

we are standing. in the shadows. of bare branches.
staring at a stump. sprayed. florescent orange.

remember the wind we had? I say.
on this spot. on Tuesday.

there. stood a tree.

II

further. down river. the bleached trunk.
of a black spruce. wind-twisted. split.

its surface inscribed. with. the fate. that befell it.
beetle writing. under living lichen. still thriving.

in the soft bank. a single leaf. from last autumn.
still in the early stages. of becoming. fossil.

in the cliff face. above. layers. of mudstone.
interspersed. with layers. of ancient ash.

drying. cracking. crumbling.
some volcanoes. never stop erupting.

II

melting. revealing. winter's machinations.
massive logs. pushed further. down river.

X marks the spot. where ice.
intends. on breaking.

ice teaching me. how it's formed.
by way. of how it's melting.

dripping. pooling. puddling.
ponding. rotting. rivering.

||

sunny. fifteen degrees. spring sings.
the simple song. of the chickadees.

fee-bee. fee-bee. come see me.
a minor 3rd. descending in pitch.

a lucid pause. between intervals.
the value. of a half note. well sustained.

11

a low slant. of prairie style.
a low bank. of clouds pile.

this is a protected tree, a sign says.
this is a human ecology.

knots. and rings. and bands. of blue paint.
on bark. and other. distinguishing features.

of decomposition. of trunks. and stumps. of trees.
and oblivious. and gregarious. as you please.

around the edges. of puddles.
flock muddles. of waxwings.

11

in an online meeting. with a colleague. in England.

how's the weather in Edmonton?

it's raining!

even I am bemused by my enthusiasm.

for wet. in a dry place.

for green. in the yellow grass.

for red. in the dogwood.

gleaming.

11

cold. flat. light. grey sky.
snow in the air.

and then. out of nowhere.
a chickadee. coming right at me.

and then another. finally. after weeks.
of being blanked. by cliquish young ones.

some grown-ups. who know. what to do.
about a peanut. who might. even. know me.

why yes I am at the wondering if I exist in the mind
of a small songbird stage of the pandemic.

and what of it.
here. have a walnut.

11

an excursion. to Whitemud Creek. with old woman bear.
to see what the beavers have been up to.

and the moose. and the wind. moving trees around.
each according. to their own principles.

and the creek itself. carving. and the wind.
and the mudstone. eroding. into hoodoos.

squinting. into bare branches. budding.
young chickadees. flitting. flirting. perching.

to each their own worshipping.
the warming. the opening.

the arc. of the wing.
the blaze. of the orb.

avem ovum orbis solis

get a load of us.
pretending to know Latin.

| |

bright inside. bite outside.
bone dry. breeze bracing.

is this sky blue enough.
does this sound crow enough.

    caw-caw-caw-caw-koodle-yah.
    koodle-yah (trilly voice)

walks this path. tall enough.
are these wings. wide enough.

how many photos. of solar halos.
and mid-sky rainbows. is enough. is enough.

    (don't ask me.)
    (I don't know yet.)

II

this soft ice. a magnet.
a channel. of open water.

tracing. racing. the far shore.
and the shouts. of an EMS crew.

melting is messy. a man went through.
yesterday. and hasn't come out yet.

the sun keeps coming. anyway.
out with the buds. out with the pollen.

out with the spruce gum. out with.
old woman bear. walking. on the flat.

talking. about the man. presumed drowned.
how cold. the water is. how stunning.

sitting. with the trees for a bit.
in a place we've never been.

listening. to the thunderbirds.
to the rain starting.

turning. to swirling.
pretending. it's not snow.

II

almost muggy. in the valley.
the city. has surreptitiously.

replaced. the ravens. with crows.
and the geese. with gulls.

listening. for chickadees. over the racket.
or under. as the case may be.

the young ones. are getting bolder.
I'm a lousy whistler. but I'm practicing.

fee-bee. fee-bee. don't laugh.
I think. they know. what I mean.

11

light. finding lichen.
shelf fungi. and birch bark.

rips. tears. curls.
and lenticels. porous tissues.

providing pathways.
for the exchange. of gases.

between internal.
and outer atmospheres.

and other abrasions.
of a less reciprocal nature.

11

brilliant. blue sky. advancing.
rotten. river ice. retreating.

walking. the slant slope.
the slick bank. above the muck mark.

roots. raw. where winter gnashed them.
and signs of beaver. busy as.

a man painting. towards the far shore.
a crowd. of gossips. gathering.

speculating. on the fire rescue crew.
down by the slipway.

a dog. this time.
lost. 30 pounds. black.

11

looking for something? someone asks me.
a chickadee. comes promptly. to hand.

this is incredible.
someone else says, in passing.

II

awake since five. since before sunrise.
eyes burning. under blue skies. sun blazing.

poplars fluffing. is an entire season.
here in the unceded territory.

of the poplar nation.
perhaps best. not to mention.

the suggestion. of flurries. forecast.
or the brief interval. of hail. we just had.

better. to focus on the river. running full throttle.
open water. and sâkipakâw. budding into catkin.

awaiting. the chickadees. fluff under-feather.
whistling. fee-bee. come see me.

below boss crow. on high branch.
screaming. bloody murder.

11

a venture. into the interior.
flummoxed. by the vernacular.

architecture. knackered by weather.
white picket fences. paint peeling.

garage door hinges. only half rusting.
a hare stares. at a piece of plywood.

a paper lantern. for no reason.

11

twenty degrees.
a gentle breeze.

a snake. in the leaves.
a squint. in the sun.

a squabble. of gulls.
guarding. the last ice islands.

a squelch. in the muck.
and now we know.

where flies come from.

11

the river cliffs again. the view up at them.
possible. from the beach again.

and the beach also. I hasten.
to mention. discernible again.

the fine line. between silt.
and surface tension.

open water again.
and cumulus.

with heat in.
a season.

11

neck aching. from craning. at solar halos.
eye watering. from squinting. at ice glinting.

light reflecting. refracting. dispersing. in high cirrus.
a low cloud. of gulls hangs. loud. over the poplars.

ear altering brain. there's a car alarm sounding.
eye saying. look! we're standing. between a stereo pair.

of dark-eyed juncos. cross calling. over the valley.
until one of them. drops down. silent. into it.

11

in my hand. a microclimate. of feet and feathers.
a flutter of wing. a double. of fingers.

and in the bush. a drip. of gum.
liquid spruce. holding. sun.

11

if all the drakes are heading one way,
old woman bear says.

then the nests are behind them.
we let them. divert our attention.

just waiting.
for rain now.

for the trees.
to explode.

11

an excursion. to elk island.
to visit the bison.

we saw dozens. of beaver houses.
in the beaver hills. but no beavers.

it being their weekend off,
we reasoned.

these bins aren't bear proof,
old woman bear says.

laughing her head off.

11

cloud sketches. in blue sky.
greater scaup. in blue pond.

or possibly lesser. or further.
of the too far from my phone family.

common golden eye. and diving.
and diving. a sleek muskrat.

the chickadees. just showing off now.
flying sideways. into tender. green light.

standing. in sound spaces. between poplars.
listening. the yellow bird again. the black crows.

angry. at a white man. drumming.
until finally. someone makes him stop.

||

the snake again, I exclaim.

as if there's only one.

eccentric.

as I'm walking alone.

||

it's raining. properly.
drenching. grass glistening.

lichen gleaming. and even.
an indecent hint. of a peony.

green. creeping. into the valley.
light slanting. through spruce leaning.

tender. fresh poplar. leaves.
doubled. in size. since yesterday.

old woman bear pauses.
to speak to them. in her language.

the river valley can hear nêhiyawêwin.
better than anything.

11

bees bumble. low. in high wind.
finally. finding some blossom.

orange kayaks. fly by.
fast. on open water.

the drift. of wood. the shingle. of shallows.
the fine line. between mudstone. and mud.

pausing. to examine. trickster pieces.
of non-fossilised wood.

then finding. three pieces.
of actual fossilised wood.

and leaving them.
for the river to carry on with.

ascending. into living wood.
of the same species.

new green. in new leaves.

the scent. of balsam poplar.

what's seventy million years.

difference. among friends.

11

great skies lately. clouds form shapely.
stately. weather coming in. from westerly.

a faint. solar halo. glows momentarily.
the far bank greening. the near bank also.

presumably. but I can't see.
the poplars. for their leaves.

unfolding. wild roses.
springing. into action.

and blooming. full. on the horizon.
sâkipakâwipîsm. leaf-budding moon.

11

it might rain, I say. that's okay.
just a short walk, old woman bear decides.

passing. between showers. stopping. to admire.
every single bud. catkin. and blossom.

of chokecherry. sour cherry.
and saskatoon berry.

stalking. feral blossom. of lilac. an invasive species.
seeds blown. from lawns. over the road.

and hedges. of hardy caragana.
first planted. by settlers. to shelter cattle.

put that in your mouth, old woman bear says.
the yellow flowers. taste slightly sweet.

white pine. is used in ceremony.
but it's not indigenous either.

neither is dandelion.

nor lily. of the valley.

we stumble. into a hidden glen of them.

a carpet. of white flowers. bowed heads.

someone walked along here, and they spread.

old woman bear says. a rhizomatic. act of magic.

11

a fold. of cloud.
over the city.

a flap. of geese.
over the territory.

a squeeze of leaves.
effecting an obliteration.

of winter sky's.
open. blue spaces.

a tangle. of life.
through which.

the winged. among us.
dart. with precision.

describing vivid worlds.
about which.

the rest of us.
know. nothing.

11

can't focus. inside. on sleeping.
waking. working. writing.

but outside. no cheep. squeak.
rustle. creak. escapes my attention.

willow catkins. squiggle twigs.
bearing froth blossoms.

heard a yellow bird.
not pictured. not big.

saw a goose wing lift.
to reveal. several goslings.

thesis

weeping willow catkins and goslings are
close relations

II

spring. so. slow. here.
and then. so sudden.

here. I thought. I'd been attending.
to the change. so obvious. to sense.

how did it happen then. how did I miss.
these increments. of green expansion.

an incursion. of fresh foliage.
an abundance. of fresh blossom.

the leafing. expanding.
filling. into every opening.

marvellous. multitudinous.
to the point. of bewildering.

11

does not each bud. deserve attention.
observation. of its progression.

from cellular. to miniature.
to full blown. constellation.

or maybe. what's wanted. here.
is privacy. to leave.

well enough.
alone.

c o d a.

the river organises the world. according to its own principles. soft bank goes with black spruce goes with leaning into vast open. sky goes with wind goes with migration. birds go with going and coming and singing. cliff goes with crumbling. sending fossils and pebbles tumbling. into riverbed bending. widening. deepening. water a colour I used to have a suit in. swift-flowing goes with a double scull skimming. oar goes with hull goes with wake goes with wash. a slosh. a scum. of orange needles. goes with fat curdles. of Styrofoam. and three pink and yellow ear plugs. an odd number. a condom. goes with the ghost. of a mask. last year's red leaf goes with this morning's white feather. light goes with shallow goes with lapping. goes with arranging. sticks. of all sizes. into neat rows. parallel to the shore. twig goes with twig goes with twig. on a flat stone. a muskrat. head smashed. goes with a parallelogram of coal. slick wet black. against dark brown mud. goes with mudstone. wet goes with rippling. dry goes with cracking. weather goes with everything. body goes with breathing. time goes with layering. slow goes with progress. pause goes with place. goes with now. goes with here.

ACKNOWLEDGEMENTS.

this writing is born of a sustained engagement with kisiskâciwan-isîpiy (the North Saskatchewan River) as it flows east through amiskwacîwâskahikan (Edmonton), in Treaty 6 Territory, Métis Region No. 4. this is the territory of the Papaschase Cree and the homeland of the Métis Nation. this is the territory of the poplar, silver birch, black spruce, tamarack, willow, and wild mountain ash. this is the homeland of the beaver, moose, muskrat, coyote, nuthatch, and chickadee nations. this is a traditional gathering place for the Cree, Blackfoot, Metis, Nakota Sioux, Iroquois, Dene, Ojibway/ Saulteaux/Anishinaabe, Inuit, and many others travellers, including swallows, red-winged blackbirds, bohemian waxwings, and trumpeter swans.

this writing began during my time as writer in residence in the English and Film Studies Department at the University of Alberta 2020-2021. all the buildings were closed, and gatherings were restricted, due to Covid.

thanks to Marilyn Dumont and the entire WRITE committee for trusting me, and thanks to all the students, faculty, and members of the public encountered so generously online.

thanks to Christine Stewart for engaging in a sustained daily writing practice with me from November 2020 to May 2021, through which the bulk of this writing was generated.

thanks to Marilyn Arsem for inspiring this daily writing practice in an online workshop in October 2020, and thanks Natalie Loveless for hosting this workshop.

thanks to notokwew muskwa manitokan (old woman bear sitting next to the creator) for sharing long walking, talking, listening, and laughing with me.

thanks to Mariléne Oliver, Ragnar Poulsen, Thomas, Tobias, and Pablo for opening their home to me.

thanks to Darren Hagen for friendship and collaboration.

thanks to elisabeth belliveau for the long phone calls, picnic table parties, and perfect snack packs.

thanks to Kelly for the crampons.

thanks to Jordan Abel and Chelsea Novak for pod picnics, epic sandwiches, and walks under the poplars with Lil Pho.

and thanks to Tonia Harris for teaching me chickadee.

four poems in this collection were longlisted for the CBC Poetry Prize 2021. excerpts of this manuscript were published in *Journal of Visual Art Practice Volume 22, 2023 - Issue 2-3: Situations of Writing*, and *Measures of Weather*.

this writing was furthered by a Visiting Fellowship from the Eccles Centre for American Studies at the British Library in London, UK, 2021, and by a week in a Leighton Studio at The Banff Centre in Treaty 7 Territory, 2023.

LAY OUT YOUR UNREST

www.ingramcontent.com/pod-product-compliance
Lightning Source LLC
Chambersburg PA
CBHW032231080426
42735CB00008B/809